for [...] little book
2 very special
People
"They followed the Lamb
Whithersoever He went"
Our love in Christ,
Clyde & Diana

In The
FOOTPRINTS
of the
LAMB

In The
FOOTPRINTS
of the
LAMB

G. Steinberger

Translated from the Norwegian edition by
Bernhard Christensen

BETHANY HOUSE PUBLISHERS
MINNEAPOLIS, MINNESOTA 55438

In the Footprints of the Lamb
G. Steinberger

Library of Congress Catalog Card Number 78–73416

ISBN 0–87123–237–5

Copyright © 1936
The Lutheran Free Church
Publishing Company
Minneapolis, Minnesota

Published by Bethany House Publishers
A Ministry of Bethany Fellowship, Inc.
11300 Hampshire Avenue South
Minneapolis, Minnesota 55438

Printed in the United States of America

FOREWORD

[Written for the Norwegian edition]

I know of no devotional book which I have re-read so many times. It is to an unusual degree filled with the words of eternal life. Through many years of bitter suffering its author learned to see the Savior as the Lamb of God, and himself to walk the pathway "in the footprints of the Lamb."

O. Hallesby
Vinderen, February, 1915

Twenty years ago I wrote the foreword given above, for the first edition of this book. Today I have nothing to subtract from that recommendation, nor anything to add to it. I desire only that the book with its quiet streams of blessing may find its way onward and inward to the suffering souls of men.

O. Hallesby
Vinderen, March, 1935

CONTENTS

The Way 11

The Light on the Way 29

The Goal of the Way 73

He That Cometh 81

These are they that follow the Lamb whithersoever he goeth.—Revelation 14:4

"This way is called: In the Footprints of the Lamb. There we learn to understand the meaning of the Cross, to comprehend its power, and to walk in its shadow. . . . The deepest meaning of the Cross is to give up one's own 'I'."

The Way . . .

These are they that follow the Lamb whithersoever he goeth. — Rev. 14:4.

The footprints of the Lamb of God mark out the only way upon which true spiritual progress is possible. It is the pathway where we find enduring peace, where we live a fruitful life, where we win spiritual victories, where we attain to the goal of glory. He who follows the Lamb in His way comes at last to where the Lamb Himself is. And the Lamb is in the midst of the throne. No other way leads thither.

Often the way of full salvation through Christ is proclaimed—and this we must continue faithfully to do—but the way in which such a saving faith can be realized in practical daily living has been far less adequately set forth. This way is the Way of the Lamb.

We ourselves often do not really understand our own life, we do not understand our own pathway; we "buffet the air" again and again as long as we have not learned to know the secret of the Lamb

11

and His way of life. Even before Pentecost, Peter was a zealous and honest soul, but he did not understand that the Master had to live and die as a *Lamb*. Therefore, it was that he denied Him.

In the Christian life our relation is to a Person, not to a doctrine. He left us an *example*. We may be led astray by doctrines, and we may grow weary of them, but we never grow weary of looking up to the Lamb and walking in His footsteps. Let us through all eternity worship the Father because He has given us the Lamb, not only as an offering for sin, but also as a *guide!* And how blessed this is for us, especially in our time when so many conflicting voices call: "Here is the Christ!" and "Lo! He is there!"

1. The Way of the Lamb is first of all a prepared Way.

The Savior's holy feet once walked upon it. Even though at times it may seem veiled and shadowy, it is nevertheless opened and made ready by Him, and this is sufficient for us. The Way therefore is not an unknown one, for all along it we see the Master's own footprints. In all our difficulties—at home, in the world, in poverty, in lowliness—everywhere we see the prints of His feet. He is "acquainted with all our ways" (Ps. 139:3). "For in that he himself hath suffered being tempted, he is able to succor them that are tempted" (Heb. 2:18).

On this Way the soul no longer complains: "I

am not understood! I am judged unfairly!" He, our High Priest, understands us, and this brings peace to our hearts. The sheep does not seek to be known and understood by others than its shepherd; it is enough for it to see his footprints, and hear his voice. When we follow the Lamb, there is nothing which can stand in our way or hinder our progress.

What we need in order to go up to Jerusalem (Matt. 21:1-3), that is, what we need in order to walk the way of death, will in the last analysis be a matter of our own choice. If we are willing to follow the Lamb, our paths will everywhere be prepared, for in every place and along every road there is abundant opportunity to die to self. He who seeks this will never be disappointed. He will find what he seeks; and this is the secret of happiness.

He who follows the Lamb has once and for all given up his own will, his own ways. He has no purposes and interests of his own. He allows his Shepherd to cancel his own wishes and plans. He observes and understands that on this way there is no longer room for a self-possessed life; and he who passes judgment upon his own life and gives it up can easily be tolerant toward the life of others! Hence, in this way one does not so easily take offense. When we stumble because of others we are not walking in the footsteps of the Lamb, we are not children of the day but of the night (John 11:9-10). To say that this or that person stands in my way is just as absurd as to say that this or that person prevents the sun from shining upon me.

Concerning this problem in the Christian life someone has said, "A Christian never feels himself misunderstood, no true Christian is ever 'neglected.' On the contrary, a Christian knows that *he* daily neglects many things in his relation to others." He who follows the Lamb cannot expect to be understood by all. There are ways in which the believer must walk alone with his God. When Abraham went with his son up to Mount Moriah, he went alone. He left his wife at home and his servants at the foot of the mountain. None of them would have understood the way he was to walk. Therefore he did not say that he was going away to sacrifice, but to worship. But what do *we* say in a similar situation? Let us be honest, and admit that we no longer understand the Way of the Lamb! We are like the children who at Christ's entry into Jerusalem cried, "Hosanna! Hosanna!" but did not realize that the King would have to go out through another gate of the city to die on the cross, and that He calls us out with Him to share His reproach (Heb. 13:13).

The first Christians were much better acquainted with this Way because they saw many who walked in it, some who with joy sold their possessions and parted them to all, others who dwelt in caves and dens and gave up not only their possessions but also their lives. For they did not wish to be above the Lamb. The vine branches are known by their oneness with the vine itself. Pierce the vine or the branch at any point, and everywhere there flows the same life-giving sap. That which makes our union with the Savior and our "abiding in Him" so difficult is that we desire to go another way. And yet there is no more blessed way on earth than the pathway of the Lamb. "Thy paths drop fatness" (Ps. 65:11).

2. The Way of the Lamb brings us abiding peace.

There we find rest. We find peace in the same degree that we follow Him. And we retain it as long as we are one with Him. This peace is not something we must strive or pray for; it is given to us as soon as we take His yoke upon us and follow Him (Matt. 11:29). The Bible distinguishes between "peace *with* God" (Rom. 5:1) and the "peace *of* God" (Phil. 4:7). These two are not the same. Peace with God, or peace in one's conscience, is a gift God gives to the sinner as soon as He comes to the cross; the peace of God, or peace in one's heart, is a blessing one receives through obedience to God's commandments (Isa. 48:18). Jesus also distinguishes between these two experiences in His well-known invitation to those who are weary (Matt. 11:28-29). He speaks first of the rest which He will give to those who *come* to Him, and then of the rest which is found by those who *follow* Him.

In the Way of the Lamb we find a peace which

abides, because there we learn to let Him deal not
only with our sins but also with our difficulties,
whether these concern our own person, our family,
or some work which rests upon us in the Kingdom
of God. Thus did Mary. She allowed Jesus to step in
and answer her sister's complaint (Luke 10:38-42).
And later, when Judas spoke his accusing words,
she again allowed the Master to answer on her behalf (John 12:1-5). To be converted to God and still
to be troubled with cares, with envy, or with a
wounded spirit, is something entirely unnatural.
Such souls lack that peace of heart which not only
passes all understanding but also conquers every
trial. Paul writes to the Thessalonians, "Now the
Lord of peace himself give you peace at all times in
all ways" (II Thess. 3:16). Can He really give peace
in *all* ways? Yea, certainly! He can give peace
through both the bitter and the sweet, through
storm and calm, through adversity and prosperity.
He Whom we follow is the Lord of Peace. As long
as we seek peace outside Him we may lose it at any
moment, or it may at least be disturbed. But the
peace which can be disturbed is not real peace. For
the true Christian, years may come and go, his con-
ditions of living may alter, but never his peace. This
changes no more than does Jesus Himself. Oh, may
we never doubt the possibility of possessing such a
peace, nor be afraid to walk in the Way where it is
found!

This Way is called: *In the Footprints of the*

Lamb. There we learn to understand the meaning of the cross, to comprehend its power, and to walk in its shadow. The deepest meaning of the cross is to give up "one's own 'I' ." Only when this dark tyrant has been wounded unto death can undisturbed peace rule. And then we no longer seek to preserve that which is condemned to death. We desire no longer, like Martha, to maintain our own authority; we gladly lay the government upon His shoulder, Who is called the Prince of Peace (Isa. 9:6). Then our peace grows ever deeper and greater. For as far as His government extends, so far extends also our peace. Jesus lived not for Himself but for His heavenly Father. For this reason His peace remained unbroken when His own received Him not, when they were ready to stone Him, and even when they nailed Him to the cross of shame.

3. On the Way of the Lamb we live a fruitful life.

Jesus served us through His words. He served us with His holy life. But above all He served us as the Lamb. As the grain of wheat which allowed itself to be laid in the earth to die, He bore much fruit. Made perfect through suffering and crowned by death, He brought many sons to glory (Heb. 2). As a dying Lamb He became a perfect Savior; without the suffering of death He would never have been this. Try only to imagine His life apart from His character as a Lamb. What would then remain of Him? A prophet mighty in word and deed, as the Emmaus disciples said. But as such He could not save us.

Similarly, try to imagine the character of the Lamb apart from *your* life! How much remains then of your Christianity? Only as a Lamb could Jesus serve and save. Only as lambs can we serve, and help our brethren to be saved. Therefore Jesus sent His disciples out as lambs. Lambs are fruitful because they give up their own and allow that which is their own to be taken from them. "A sheep before its shearers is dumb" (Isa. 53:7).

Fruit is more than profit. Fruit reproduces itself. We can tell whether or not our teaching and our life are light by whether or not they create and ripen spiritual fruit in others. Only where there is life can there be fruit; and, according to John 6:47-59, life, eternal life, exists only where one has been willing to die together with the Lamb. For the greatest victory of our Lord is when He finds on earth those who share His death with Him. Such persons teach by visible example, the type of teaching we all know to be the most effective.

Today a minister wrote me: "I can only be of blessing to my congregation when I live Christ before their eyes. I believe that this is the most effective kind of preaching. It has always attracted me personally and it still continues to do so. He who thirsts, gladly refreshes himself at a cool flowing fountain. And are not we called to be 'fountains'?" Yes, *wells* of living water! (John 4:14).

It is not enough that we have life; we must have it more abundantly (John 10:10 and 7:37). But the life of Christ can be revealed only by those who have died and whose "life is hid with Christ in God" (Col. 3:3). In Isaiah 53:11, it is said concerning the Lamb that "He shall see of the travail of his soul and shall be satisfied." Here we have *hidden* travail and *visible* fruit. The followers of the Lamb can do this type of work because they are willing to live a hidden life, and because they, as followers of the Lamb, have the heart of a shepherd. How deeply we need such persons as can do hidden soul-work! These give strength, poise, and blessing to all our public activity. One soon notices the effect in a congregation where no one lives a life of prayer.

"I would gladly do something for the Lord," said a Christian to me, "but I am deaf, and therefore I cannot associate with people."

I answered, "Speak to your God about these souls, speak to Him in secret, and He shall reward you openly."

Do you know how the Lamb received the seed of creative spiritual power? "He made his soul an offering for sin" (Isa. 53:10). That is, He took upon Himself the guilt of others and bore it as though it were His own. So also did Ezra, Nehemiah, and Daniel. They said, "We have sinned!" That is the Way of the Lamb.

As a lamb one can do every type of work. No

work is too humble for the lambs, for all they do is done to the glory of God. Many a daughter would win her mother more quickly for Jesus if she, instead of constantly telling her that she should be converted, would wash the dishes for mother, clean up the house, and thereby show her what conversion really is. We have enough people to do great things; but who is willing to do the *little* things? Begin with the little things, and you will not only find enough work but also harvest a blessing.

In Exodus 12 we read: "They shall take to them every man a lamb for a household." Each of you must see to it that a lamb is provided for your household. How can this be done? When we rejoice in the Lamb at home! And when is this possible? When we ourselves are as lambs. The spirit of the lamb is always attractive, and its nature is victorious over all obstacles. We read in Isaiah 42 concerning the Lamb of God, "He will not fail nor be discouraged, till he hath set justice in the earth." How did He accomplish this? Not by words, but by a sacrifice: "Him who knew no sin he made to be sin on our behalf." How do you "set justice" in your own home? When you, without murmuring, can give up your own rights. I know a widow with ten children who are all converted to God. Her home is a bit of heaven on earth. In it there is never heard scolding, complaining, or imperious commands. Each member of the home reads the desire of the others in their eyes. And how has this home become thus? Not by words, for the mother has never said to the children, "You must be converted." By self-denial and unselfish living she has made the Lamb to be precious to her loved ones. I visit this home as often as I can, though not in order to instruct, but to learn.

4. On the Way of the Lamb one wins a victor's crown.

It was as a lamb that our Savior conquered, not as the Lord of heaven and earth, "who spoke and it was done, who commanded and it stood fast." He sent His disciples out as lambs to overcome a world which knew Him not but was bitterly opposed to Him—and they conquered it! When Jacob was overcome, he conquered and became an Israel. To be weak is not the same as to stumble and to fall, but it is rather to be helpless and without defense, to be nothing in one's self. Then there is room for the power of God. In I Corinthians 1:25 Paul says that "the weakness of God is stronger than men." Here weakness is attributed to God. "When I am overcome, he is my helper," says David. God always takes the part of the weak. There is a holy way in which to be defeated; one can suffer defeat for God's sake. Mary submitted to her sister, Martha. She remained patient when the latter rebuked her. Hannah submitted to the taunts of Peninnah; she allowed herself to be abused. Jesus' whole life, from His first day to the death on the cross, was nothing else than submission, but He endured it for God's sake. And step by step it brought victory to His side. It was therefore that "the grace of God was upon him" so mightily, and God was His unfailing help. Thus He went from victory to victory; and where He descended to the deepest depths, He won the most perfect and glorious victory. With nail-pinioned hands and feet, but with a heart full of obedience, He conquered sin, and the world, and hell.

On Mount Zion, where as the most despised and scorned He suffered defeat, John saw Him stand as the Lord of Victory, and at His side the fruit of His death, a hundred and forty and four thousand in whose foreheads His and the Father's name are written. Where you today allow yourself to be "overcome" for His sake, you will sooner or later receive the fruits of victory. When Joseph was sent to prison, when Daniel was cast into the lions' den and his friends condemned to the fiery furnace, they did not appear to be victors, yet such they were. Here God's weakness was stronger than men, stronger than an empire of a hundred and twenty provinces. And what was revealed in the garden of Gethsemane, before the council of the Jews, before Pilate's judgment-seat, in the hands of the soldiers, and on the cross? God's weakness, which is stronger than men, yea, stronger than all the kingdom of death!

In Hebrews 11 we are given a vision of the heroes of faith. The first had to give up his life because his brother hated him, and concerning the last ones we are told: "They were stoned, they were sawn asunder, they were tempted, they were slain with the sword, they went about in sheepskins, in goat-skins; being destitute, afflicted, ill-treated, wandering in deserts and mountains and caves." Were these heroes? Yes, in the judgment of God! It is written that they "from weakness were made strong" (v. 34). What does this mean? Through suffering they became able to bear much suffering; by enduring they were made strong to endure; by being defeated they learned to conquer. Because Jesus for three whole years had endured Judas, He could cry out from the cross, "Father, forgive them." Because He had experienced being denied by His own, He could bear to be denied by a whole people. Thus did the Lamb become a lion.

5. The Way of the Lamb is the only way to glory.

Because Jesus humbled Himself He was exalted. Four steps downward led Him up to glory. We read in Philippians 2:6-9:

1. He gave up the privilege of equality with God;
2. He humbled Himself;
3. He became obedient unto death;
4. Yea, even the death of the cross!

"Wherefore also God highly exalted him, and gave unto him the name which is above every name." That was *His* way to glory, and for us, too, there is no other way. Only the way in the footprints of the Lamb leads to the throne; to be glorified as the Lamb, is to become like the Lamb. We cannot become like Him as God's Son, as the King of heaven and earth, but we are called to be like Him in being as lambs. He is the pattern according to which God molds us.

When God planned to create man, He said, "Let us make man in our image after our likeness." The image that resembles Him, the Son of Man, is God's ideal. And from this ideal He has never turned away. In Revelation 19 we see it realized. There a great multitude is seen standing by the side of the Lamb as His bride, in appearance like unto Himself. We have often stopped with justification, but God does not stop here. Those "whom he called, them he also justified: and whom he justified, them he also glorified" (Rom. 8:30). How glorious is God's thought for us: that we are to be "conformed to the image of his Son"! (Rom. 8:29). How do we attain to this? We are given the answer in the same chapter: "And we know that to them that love God all things work together for good" (v. 28). They know that the Lord's hand guides their way and that He leads them only in paths that are necessary for their discipline and growth. They know that only those shall stand by the side of the Lamb who dare to follow Him. Therefore they walk in His way, even if it should be said concerning them, "We were accounted as sheep for the slaughter" (Rom. 8:36). They do not seek gifts and blessedness; they seek only Him. They say with Asaph, "Whom have I in heaven but thee? And there is none upon earth that I desire besides thee" (Ps. 73:25).

For the people of Israel the desert was the way to glory, but because they were not willing to follow their God through hardships and trials, the glory departed from them. In the moment that the glory of God's people should have been most clearly revealed, they murmured and set themselves up against His will, grieving the Holy Spirit. Israel was called to be an example of God's faithfulness and power to all coming generations. But they fell short of attaining to God's purpose for them; they were not willing to put their trust in God when they walked through the darkness, and therefore would not follow Him through hours of tribulation either. Has God led you out into the desert? Has He plucked from under your feet all that you depended upon? Then a glorious experience is yours! See if this be not a way whereby God will glorify you! Do not complain about what you have lost, and do not yearn to have it given back again, for then you are like Israel who wished to turn back to Egypt. God will lead you on further. Instead of the fleshpots He gives you bread from heaven, and instead of water from the Nile, water from the rock. But you must put your trust in Him also in the desert, and through days of darkness and difficulty. This is possible, however, only for those who have lost their self-assurance in the desert whereto God beckons His children.

Out upon these ways God does not *force* His children. He *allures* them. "Therefore, behold, I will allure her, and bring her into the wilderness, and speak comfortably unto her. And I will give her her vineyards from thence, and the valley of Achor for a door of hope; and she shall make answer there, as in the days of her youth, and . . . thou shalt call me 'my husband' . . . and I will break the bow and the sword and the battle out of the land, and will make them to lie down safely" (Hosea 2:14-19). What did Israel find upon this way? She found greater riches, a living hope, an undisturbed joy, a deeper understanding, a more inclusive peace, an unbroken security, a deeper soul-cleansing, and the most intimate fellowship with her God. Can this be called a desert? Not by those who like Moses, see beyond reproach, the reward; who like David, see beyond suffering, the Savior; who like Jesus, see beyond the cross, the crown (Heb. 12:2). What do you see beyond disgrace, beyond suffering, beyond the cross? Do you see the widening vistas of glory that lie beyond all these?

When Judas went out, determined to betray Jesus, and the bitterest drop fell into the Savior's chalice of suffering, He said, "Now is the Son of Man glorified, and God is glorified in him" (John 13:31). Glorified through suffering! Every pathway seeking to avoid the suffering which God has sent involves just that much lost glory. "God giveth grace to the humble." Every time we turn away from an experience of humbling, we turn away from His grace. How much glory and grace we have already missed. Jesus did not turn aside, in the hour of darkness, but laid His agony in the Father's hand in order that He might not lose the blessing that lay therein. In John 17 He says, "Father, the hour is come; glorify thy Son." What hour was this? It was the bitter hour in Gethsemane and on Calvary. What did He expect from this hour? Transfiguration, glory! Nor has He been disappointed in that expectation. What infinite glory Gethsemane and Golgatha have brought to Him! Millions of creatures in heaven, on earth, under the earth, and in the sea sing a new song: *Worthy is the Lamb that was slain*!

Do you also have hours of darkness and bitterness? What do you expect from them? That they shall pass as swiftly as possible? It is not for this reason that they are given to you, but that they may bring you a new glory. These are sacred experiences! Be very careful, therefore, with yourself and others. Run not away from the heavenly Jeweller's work, for in just such hours the diamond's facet attains a new brilliance that it may shine yet more clearly thereafter. What radiance was brought to Daniel by the den of lions, to his friends by the fiery furnace, to Hannah by her patience with Peninnah, and to Mary by her silence! In Proverbs 4:18 we read, "But the path of the righteous is as the dawning light, that shineth more and more unto the perfect day." The steps whereby Joseph went down into prison have surely greater radiance for us than his steps upward to the throne of a king. That which makes the men of God so great and impressive is not, first and foremost, what they have accomplished. It is rather how they are able, by God's help, to pass through the greatest difficulties and the darkest hours; when, like Abraham, they give God the dearest they have; when, like Daniel, they brave the greatest dangers; and when like Moses, they endure that which is well nigh impossible. Thus they glorify God. That is the glory which the child of God constantly seeks. Glory for himself he does not desire.

The Light on the Way . . .

The Lamb is the light thereof. — Rev. 21:23.

Let the Lamb be our light today, for "in his light we see light." From this day forth, let us enter His school; for the place which God has pointed out to His saints is at Jesus' feet (Deut. 33:3). The "saints" are they who are given to God and who have given themselves to God. Let us come to Him as such, learn of Him, and walk in His way.

1. The Lamb teaches you to love.

"Having loved his own that were in the world, he loved them unto the end" (John 13:1). How did He love? He loved His own more than Himself, and this is really the "love of Christ." Natural love loves according to its own inclination; the love which the Law commands loves because God wills it. It loves from duty and loves its neighbor as itself (Luke 10:27). But the love of Christ loves others more than itself. How far we still come short of that! So many times we have begun to love, but have soon grown weary and proved unfaithful to the sacred task. Only in the school of Christ do we learn the true meaning of love. There we learn to love in *God's* way, to love with that love which is in God's own heart. There is no place where sin creeps in more frequently than in the realm of affection. One does less harm by hatred than by false love. Often our enemies have not hurt us so much as our "good friends." If we desire that our inward man shall grow and prosper, then let us undertake a thorough-going investigation of ourselves and allow our hearts to be cleansed of all impurity. In the great chapter on love we are told that "love rejoices in the truth."

Love is truth! Love constantly seeks the eternal in its neighbor, and it points toward this with gentleness and seriousness, and even, if necessary, with unswerving insistence. Carnal love is blind, but divine love has an open eye for truth. Carnal love loves in order to be loved. True love loves without expecting any gratitude. It does not consider what it can achieve for itself, but, rather, what can be produced for the Lord. True love seeks from Jesus only Himself; and from men, not their recognition, still less their money, but only their immortal soul.

Love is self-giving! It loves all the way to death, even if it is brought to the cross with the Master. Carnal love also loves unto death, yet not unto Christ's death but unto spiritual death. Alas, many friendships lead to this! Wounds are received which cannot be healed through a whole long life. Once they spoke in love to each other about all things. They could not live, if they did not see each other every day. But then after some years, the burning love turned into bitter hatred. Carnal love always ends in hatred. By carnal love is not meant sensual love, but false love among the pious.

God, in His grace, permits even a downpour of bitter, unrighteous rebukes and an icy, loveless north wind to beat upon love's edifice. The poorly-built house falls together with a crash that is heard far away. Where one ceases to love with the love of Christ, there unrighteousness, confusion, and death, are the inevitable result. And to love in God's way can be learned only in the school of the Lamb.

Love is obedience. When and how do we love in God's manner? For many, this is a burning question. In I John 5:2 we are given a striking answer: "Hereby we know that we love the children of God, when we love God and do his commandments." He who loves God will by his love bind men to God, not to himself. John rejoiced when his disciples left him and followed after Jesus, because he loved Jesus. He who keeps God's commandments, loves; for by his obedience he leads his brethren upon God's Way, and this is true love. Such a love conquers at last and is understood, even if throughout all its life it may have been regarded as harshness. Every friendship which does not rest upon this foundation is enmity. On the whole, this matter of cultivating friendship is a difficult point. It requires much grace and truth from above. Very few can say as the ancient Church Father said about himself and his friend: "We were acquainted with only two ways, the one to the Church and the one to the teachers of the Church; we spoke of only two things, God and His Word."

Love is life! Without love we cannot live. Even as our spirit is created to know, so is our heart created to love. Our heart is created for love even as the bird is created for flight. Love is our life's beginning and end. It is the soul's light and source of warmth. He who sins against love lays hands upon his own life. Love is the greatest power. Only as long as we love do we live. Where love awakens, the dark tyrant of ego dies. Love is the bond of perfectness; it comprehends all, even God. Love is the one commandment which the Lord has given His own. Love is the mark of the new birth and the proof that our faith is genuine. It is a fruit of the Holy Spirit and compensates for the presence of Jesus Himself. What is the reason that God's children have so little love? Because they have too little of the Holy Spirit. How then shall we obtain more of the Spirit? By beginning to love more. Then the Triune God places Himself on our side, for He is, above all, the God of love. "Put on therefore, as God's elect, holy and beloved, a heart of compassion" (Col. 3:12). Put on compassion and you will be as though "clad in festive garments, as though you had drunk of the wine of gladness and were refreshed by the peace of heaven, as though you had hind's feet, and arms as strong as Samson." Do you think that the Good Samaritan was a happy or an unhappy man? Who was more tired that evening, the priest or the Samaritan? Who do you suppose was the happier, he who gave away his dime or he who kept it in his pocket? Oh, you poor children of God, who stand and wait for power from above, who seek after deeper peace and richer joy! Begin to love, and you shall begin to live! The Corinthians desired to do something extraordinary. But Paul showed them a more excellent way, the way where:

Love beareth all things,
Believeth all things,
Hopeth all things,
Endureth all things.

Not only *some* things, but *all* things. No one can deny that this type of love is something extraordinary. Yet the opportunity to experience it is open to all. Faith is the beginning and love the goal of our life. Both come from God and lead to God. God has given us so rich an opportunity to achieve joy in life, just because He has given us so rich an opportunity to love. For all that calls love into service will but increase our happiness. Come, let us learn of the Lamb, that we may see what love is! Let Him be our light, Who has loved unto death! Love leads to suffering. Christ's love brought Him to the cross. Only he is able to love, therefore, who is able to suffer. As long as we expect thanks for our love, we do not love from a pure heart.

2. The Lamb teaches you to serve.

Only he who is conscious of his nobility can serve. When Jesus knew that He had gone forth from God and went to God, He laid aside His garments, took a towel and girded Himself, and served. Thereby He has given to all service a divine touch. The first principle in His life's program was this: "Not to be ministered unto, but to minister!" He who is born of God has His mind, and he who desires one day to stand by His side walks in His way. Only in the school of the Lamb does one learn to serve, and only the humble can serve. Therefore the Fathers call humility the spirit of a servant. To what end are we converted? "To serve," Paul says (I Thess. 1:9). For what shall you use your possessions? For service! Would that all converted persons knew this! Then our poor mission societies would no longer be in such need. The Bible shows us Jesus in two forms above all: that of the Servant, and that of the Lamb. "My Servant" is God's best-loved name for Him in the Old Testament.

He served us with His Word. He could refresh the weary, comfort the sorrowing, discomfit the self-assured, punish the insincere, and counsel those who went astray. "He had the words of eternal life," said Peter.

How do you speak? Can you, after you have conversed with someone, lift up your eyes and say, "Father, do Thou plant what I have said deep in his heart that it may grow and bear fruit." Or perhaps you must say, "Forgive, blot it out!" What manner of words do you use? Are they life-destroying or life-giving? None of your words is lost; they return, in one form or another, to you or to others. Miriam spoke to Aaron about her brother Moses, and together both spoke against him. First one speaks *about* his neighbor, then *against* him. Miriam poisoned Aaron's soul and caused him to sin. Oh, this passion for gossip! It is a fire that consumes, and the disease from which God's people suffer most. When you speak with your brother concerning others, do you drop a poison into his soul from which he cannot easily escape? Are the faults of others veiled by your silence or your speech? Do you help to the end that your brothers and sisters can be saved, or are the sins and passions of others aroused and nourished by your words? Do you too carry on this colportage of the devil? Because many cannot keep the tongue in check, and because God has no rein with which to bind it, He often imposes a heavy burden. And the burden of God weighs heavily upon the soul, as one soon realizes. Miriam became a leper. Thus God clearly shows that He regards slander as an abominable, stinking disease. Herein lies the secret reason why so many of God's children live a weak or a dead Christian life. The poison of gossip and the practice of judging others have slain them. Much more than we realize, we become partakers in the guilt of others because we have not learned to deal in a holy manner with their lack of holiness. But if we will attend the school of Him who called Judas "friend," and who healed Malchus's ear, we shall learn to act likewise.

He served us with His holy life. To the disciples He bequeathed an example (John 13). The apostles and the martyrs would never have died for the sake of the Gospel, if their Lord had not first died. No one would have borne the many sufferings for the Gospel's sake, if the Lord Himself had not first borne the greatest of all. What is it that robs our present-day Christianity of its radiance and compelling power? Undoubtedly it is the fact that there is so little difference between a child of God and a child of the world, in regard to love, patience, and self-denial. Life, not talk, is the light of men. That which gives life its worth is a good example. Paul never spoke with greater authority than when he could say: "Be ye imitators of me!"

God uses two means of bringing men to the light: His Holy Word, and holy men and women who live according to the Word. When the Word becomes flesh, that is, takes on human form, we behold the light of glory (John 1:14). In Christian lands, God's Word is found in almost every house, but in many places it is almost as if dead. It becomes living only when it has been released to create a holy personality. Paul would certainly have forgotten the words spoken when he argued with Stephen in the school of the Greek-speaking Jews; but Stephen's transfigured face in the hour of death, the joy which he revealed when he gave up this life, the prayer for his enemies, were all indelibly imprinted upon Paul's soul, and revealed themselves as a triumphant power of God in the persecutions that he himself had to undergo.

3. The Lamb teaches you to "endure all things."

"He bore!" we read again and again, and yet more often see. But thereby is not meant the moment when He, as the sacrificial Lamb, took the sins of men upon Himself and bore them on the cross. Here we think rather of His whole power to endure, as He allowed it to be revealed in daily living. According to His own testimony, His power consisted in the laying down of His life (John 10:17)—not in His speaking as no one had spoken before Him, nor in His feeding of the five thousand with five loaves and two small fishes, nor even in His raising of the dead. All this was power, but *His* power to endure did not only reveal itself on the cross; His whole life on earth consisted in constantly laying it down. In all His daily difficulties He offered Himself to God, driven by the Holy Spirit. Thus He was prepared for bringing the great sacrifice on the cross. To be rejected by His own people, to be misunderstood by His disciples, to be declared insane by His family, to be stamped as a dangerous fanatic by the nation's leaders—all this required great power of endurance. "And as he was, so also are we in this world." He says therefore in Revelation 3:12, "I will make him a pillar in the temple of my God." The purpose of the pillar is not decoration, but the carrying of a burden. People who desire to be admired are not pillars; they collapse as soon as there is something heavy to bear. People who are touchy are not pillars, for to be touchy is exactly the opposite of being able to endure. Very often when I stand in the railroad station and see the cars in front of me, my eye falls upon that corner of the car where it is stated that it has a capacity of bearing so and so many thousand pounds. The serious question then arises for me: "How great a capacity for bearing have you?" We need people who have this quality, especially in our Christian congregations, where the spirit of touchiness and faction so often pushes its way in. In the house of God the principle is *to remain under your burden*, even as the pillar does. In other words, be patient. Jesus conquered only as a lamb. What is it that characterizes the lamb? Both in the Old and New Testament we are told, "He endured!" Those who follow the Lamb are those who can endure. He who cannot do this does not have the Holy Spirit.

One may strike the rock, and it gives forth living water. When they struck Christ, the Rock—struck Him unto death—there flowed from Him nothing save love and life. Does there flow from us, when we are struck, living water, or the bitterness of Marah? When Stephen was stoned by his fellow-citizens, he cried out with a transfigured face, "Lord, lay not this sin to their charge!" And when Paul was rejected by his people, he could say, "I could wish that I myself were accursed from Christ for my brethren's sake, my kinsmen according to the flesh" (Rom. 9:3). Such is the power to endure! Such is Christianity! Such is grace in practice!

The Bible speaks not only of forgiveness, of preparatory and restoring grace, but also of practical grace. If we ask Peter what grace is, he answers, "For this is acceptable, if for conscience toward God a man endureth griefs, suffering wrongfully" (I Peter 2:19). Both of Peter's Epistles deal entirely with this grace. Ask the car inspector who runs along the side of the express train rolling into the station, and strikes each wheel with his hammer, "Why do you do this?" He answers, "To see if the wheel is in good condition." "How do you know when everything is in good order?" "When the tone is full and clear." To allow oneself to be struck, and at the same time to remain undisturbed, is to stand the test; this is to proclaim the wondrous light of the Gospel to the world; this is to show the world the Master. A minister whom someone had wronged said bitterly to his wife, "I shall show him who is master." "Which master?" his wife asked him gently. The minister became astonished and said, in shame, "This time I would hardly have shown him the Master, but myself." To show others the right way can only be done by walking in the footprints of the Lamb, by following Him in love and humility and faithfulness.

4. The Lamb teaches you to be humble.

"I am lowly in heart," He says; "learn of me!" "We have derived our pride from another; we must derive our humility too from another," someone has said. By nature nothing is more alien and incomprehensible to us than humility; there is therefore nothing of which we have so little. The most certain proof that we are humble is that we no longer try to avoid humiliations, that we can be grateful for them and even find joy in them. Paul's words, "I glory in my weakness," also imply, "I find joy in everything that humbles me." To that point I have not yet attained. Meanwhile I remember very clearly that moment not so long ago when for the first time I could thank the people who had humbled me. Previously I had only received and endured these humblings because they were inevitable. But Paul found joy in all which humbled him, and Peter says, "God giveth grace to the humble." Every time we avoid an experience of humbling, we miss an experience of grace. Peter says further, "Put on humility." Humility is the cloak which protects us from the cold spread by others.

What is humility? Humility is not a virtue, but rather the soil in which all other virtues thrive. No virtue which has not grown in this soil has any value. Therefore Jesus says to all who come to Him that they must first and foremost learn one thing of Him: humility! Humility is that power which can place itself in a lowly position. "He humbled himself," says Paul in Philippians 2:8. Humility leads us to feel that we ourselves are nothing, but that God is all. It seeks not its own glory but directs everything away from itself. It was in this spirit that a noted English missionary, after a bishop had eulogized him in a large gathering, simply recited the little stanza:

> Lo here I fall, my Savior,
> 'Tis I deserve Thy place;
> Look on me with Thy favor,
> Vouchsafe to me Thy grace.

Humility is the power which minimizes rather than magnifies that which it does; it does not desire to attract attention and create enthusiasm for itself. Why, may we suppose, did Jesus at the awakening of Jairus's daughter say, "She is not dead, but sleepeth"? He did not want to attract attention. To begin with, we usually make a thing look very black in order that it may seem so much whiter after we have finished with it, or we make it very small in order that it may stand forth so much larger. Humility knows nothing about itself. Nor does it know that it is humble. It is a power which can do nothing of itself; it can only humble itself and be dependent. Jesus says repeatedly, "I can do nothing of myself." "My Father is greater than all," He says in John 10. In Revelation 1:1 John shows how He is still dependent upon the Father even after He has been exalted to sit at the right hand of the Majesty on high, and has been given all power in heaven and on earth: "The Revelation of Jesus Christ *which God gave him.*"

This greater humility we see in the Triune God Himself. The Father and the Son prepared the way for the "Kingdom of the Spirit" in which we now live; the Spirit and the Bride say, "Come, Lord Jesus, come quickly." They prepare the way for the Kingdom of the Son, the Millennial Kingdom. The Son, the Spirit, and the Bride bring in the "Kingdom of the Father," where God shall be all in all, where He will be the true Father for all who are called children in heaven and on earth (Eph. 3:15). The true meaning of humility, therefore, we can learn only from Christ, who has revealed God. He who is rooted and grounded in love by faith in Christ learns to be "lowly in heart." This love is really humility. Therefore it is said concerning Jesus, "Having loved his own that were in the world, he loved them to the end." Humility is a power which can deal with those who are far below one as it deals with brethren. He was not ashamed to call His disciples brethren, even though they fled from Him in the hour of trial, and even denied Him, as Peter did. Humility is the power which can tolerate the shortcomings of others. Because He who is humble regards himself as the least worthy, he does not cherish doubts concerning others. Humility is one of the loveliest traits of the Lamb of God. Ah, seek not thou any other loveliness! Humility is the power which can show a special friendliness toward the one who has done wrong, even as the Savior showed toward Peter, "Go tell my brethren and Peter that I live." One does not help others to become humble by drawing away from them, but by loving and following after them, as Jesus did with Peter, and thus showing them the way they must go in order to learn humility.

5. The Lamb teaches you to deny yourself.

He "counted not the being on an equality with God a thing to be grasped," we read concerning Christ in Philippians 2:6. The deepest meaning of the cross is to deny one's own life. Paul expresses it thus: "He died for all, that they that live should no longer live unto themselves" (2 Cor. 5:15). We understand the meaning of the cross and experience its power only when we can say with Paul, "None of us liveth to himself" (Rom. 14:7). The fall of our first parents consisted in their making themselves the center of life. The soul who does this today will learn that spiritual darkness and death, separation from and enmity toward God, are the consequences. In all that is selfish, the power of Satan is active. In the selfish heart there burns the hidden fire of hell. As long as we cherish our own lives, we keep ourselves under God's curse; for on the cross God has cursed all that is selfish. "To live for one's self" is to be against God. Our own "I" is synonymous with "flesh," and "the mind of the flesh is enmity against God" (Rom. 8:7). Flesh is ingrown selfishness. The selfish person desires to have all things for himself, desires to be the center of all things; and when this is not possible, he draws back, deeply hurt.

Holy Scripture shows us our own "I," or the self, in six major forms, namely: self-confidence, a desire to help ourselves, self-seeking, self-will, self-satisfaction, and self-exaltation. All these together may truly be called the "thousand-headed monster," the "mother of all sin and misery," the "dark tyrant." Let us consider each of these six forms of the self-life:

a. Self-confidence. It is not enough that we commit ourselves to God; He must also be able to entrust Himself to us. In John 2:24 we are told that "Jesus did not trust himself unto them, for that he knew all men." To those who desire only to see and receive, Jesus cannot entrust Himself. Wonder is not the same as faith. When Jacob saw the ladder to heaven he marvelled at God's goodness and holiness, but he did not yet believe in them. To whom can Jesus commit Himself? To those who do not

The Light on the Way / 45

place confidence in themselves. To those who follow Him all the way to the cross, who take their stand beneath the cross, and who no longer seek after gifts and blessings, but who seek *Him* alone. John was the only disciple who followed Jesus all the way to the cross, and to him the dying Master committed the dearest He had on earth, His mother. We do not realize at all how deeply self-confidence is rooted in our hearts until that which we have consciously or unconsciously relied upon is taken away from us. Do you know why God led the people of Israel out into the wilderness? In order that they might learn to look up and to expect all things from above. In Goshen they had received what they needed from the earth; but now they found themselves in the desert with the dry hot sands under their feet, and they had to say to one another, "If we are to receive help, it must come from above." And, truly, from above came bread, meat, and even water. "Moses smote the rock and water came forth abundantly."

Thus God takes away all things from under our feet, until we have nothing left but *Him.* God has always the highest goal in view, namely, to lead us into self-denial. Everything is directed toward teaching us to entrust ourselves to Him. Therefore, we must often suffer defeat. You fight with all your might against sin and find yourself surrounded by the enemy. You pray fervently and sincerely: "O God, help me and stay by me." But it seems that

God does not hear. You cry yet more earnestly for help, but He seems to have no concern for you. Is He then really merciless? No! Just because He is merciful, He cannot help you. If He did, you would not be freed from your self-confidence; you would not learn to fight the good fight of faith and thus attain the victory which the Master has won; you would not learn to say "Jesus only!" but you would still continue to say "Jesus and I."

Peter the self-confident could not be saved, in the final analysis, except through a fall. So the Lord led him to the place where another girded him, where he allowed himself to be led, and where he stretched out his hands toward the strong, faithful, gentle shepherd-hands of his Master. It is commonly said concerning Jacob that he wrestled with God; but, upon reading Genesis 32, we find that a *man* wrestled with him. And when Jacob lay upon the ground with a strained thigh, he cried, "I will not let thee go except thou bless me!" Previously, he had always blessed himself. After Paul had been blind and helpless, he was able to say, "I can do all things." When he could do no more, he was able to do all.

b. The desire to help ourselves. Another form of our own ego is the desire to help ourselves. Nothing seems to be more difficult for our natures than to be silent and to wait; it seems much easier for us to act, even if we bring ourselves into difficulties by so doing. "Shall I smite with the sword?" we say with

Peter. "Shall we call fire down from heaven?" we ask with James and John. Saul's downfall began with his failure to wait until God came to him. Only a few hours more and the Lord would have established his kingdom forever. Even Abraham, who in the school of God had learned to wait as none other had, became guilty of this sin when he allowed Sarah to give him the Egyptian Hagar as a concubine, in order to receive by her the seed which God had promised him. As a result God was silent toward him for thirteen years. He had snatched the guidance out of the Lord's hand. In the belief that he had to help God, he wanted to shorten the time of waiting. That we are no better than Abraham, no one will doubt. Numberless times we have helped, or at least have intended to help, ourselves, thereby causing ourselves grave difficulties and grieving God.

In Psalm 37 we find three kinds of answers to prayer:
1. "Delight thyself also in the Lord; and he will give thee the desires of thy heart."
2. "Commit thy way unto the Lord; trust also in him!"
3. "Be still before Jehovah, and wait patiently for him!"

There are things which we ask for today, and tomorrow God gives them to us; there are things which we commit to God and immediately experience that He is active on our behalf; but there are also times when it is necessary to calm our souls and say, "Be still, and wait for Him." Of giving, committing, and surrendering oneself to God, the last is the most difficult. Only he who has *given* himself to God can *commit* himself to Him, and only he who has committed himself to Him can *surrender* himself to Him. One gives himself to God only once, but one commits himself to Him consciously from day to day, and thus one learns to surrender himself to God also in the evil days. Not before we exercise ourselves in faith can God test us in it. In Genesis 15 we read concerning Abraham how God tried his faith by making him wait for God while he offered his sacrifice.

Seeking to avoid difficulties is another characteristic of our desire to help ourselves. We always try to cut off, or plane away, the cross which God has given us, so that it will be lighter and easier to carry. Jesus did not do this. He bore His cross. His followers are to be known by the cross. When you cut away piece after piece of yours, there finally remains nothing of it of course, but then nothing remains of the Savior either. You say that this or that person must move out of the house because he makes life bitter for you. What is this but to cut away from the cross? You withdraw yourself because you say you are not understood. What is this but to reduce your cross? Although the Jews wanted to stone Jesus, He returned to them. And when His disciples asked in astonishment, "Goest thou thither again?" He replied, "If a man walk in the day he stumbleth not." Do not extricate yourself from rough hands. God will use them to make you perfect. Concerning Jesus, we read, "The soldiers platted a crown of thorns and put it on his head" (John 19:2). He gave His back to the smiters and He hid not His face from shame and spitting (Isa. 50:6). He had power to help Himself, but He never used it.

c. Self-seeking. A much more repulsive side of our own ego is self-seeking. This is the opposite of self-sacrifice. The self-seeking soul is a robber, for he steals from God that which belongs to Him, and takes for himself that which belongs to others. Not only does self-seeking carry on its devilish work out in the world, but also in the gatherings of religious people, in the house of the righteous, even in the hearts of those who desire to follow the unselfish Jesus. It is self-seeking when one desires to appear more pious than others, to pray more beautifully than others, when one always wants to have the advantage for oneself. But the Scriptures say: "Cursed be the deceiver" (Malachi 1:14). Many of the divisions among God's children are the result of self-seeking, the dark tyrant of the soul. Heaven would already be on earth if self-seeking were deposed from its throne.

"Go to the ant and consider her ways," says Solomon. First and foremost the ant exemplifies unselfishness. So also does the vine, which becomes fruitful only by unselfish giving its sap to the branch which then brings forth fruit. How many powers and gifts are unused, how much grace is lost, through selfishness! How much work is left undone for its sake! How many souls are lost! How many awakened ones now slumber again, because their leaders have been selfish!

Self-seeking will attempt only that which seems great, and will expect results only from persons of consequence. Its motto is: "I feel that I am sufficient in myself. Everything must exist for me, otherwise it has no value." But when love awakens in us, self-seeking dies; then the law of the flesh no longer rules, but the law of the spirit. Then we no longer ask "How much must I give up for Jesus' sake?" but "How much *may* I give up for Him who has loved me and given Himself up for me?" Self-seeking is the opposite of self-giving. Someone has said, "True self-giving constantly *seeks permission* to give itself, and counts all things to be loss which cannot be given up for Jesus' sake."

Self-seeking desires to awaken men's sympathy, can be easily insulted, expects gratitude from people, and does not permit itself to be served. The self-seeking, precious ego takes care that every eye sees, and that every ear hears *him*, "the patient sufferer," and cannot understand why everyone does not have sympathy with him. The very clearest sign of self-seeking is complaint about others.

The secret and motto of Abraham's life were contained in these four words: "I will take nothing"

(Gen. 14:23). How he practiced this in his life is suf-
ficiently well known. There too you have the solution of the secret of why God said to him, "I will
bless thee. In thee shall all the families of the earth
be blessed. I will give unto thee, and to thy seed, the
land of thy sojournings." God could do this because
Abraham sought nothing for himself. He had es-
caped from himself, and that is certainly the most
precious fruit of faith. Great was his faith, but even
greater was his unselfishness. Unselfishness is love;
for love is concerned, as we know, not with "I" but
with "you." When Paul writes the great Love
Chapter, I Corinthians 13, it would seem that he is
sketching the figure of Abraham without mention-
ing his name. For whom does the summary of the
chapter,

Love beareth all things,

Believeth all things,

Hopeth all things,

Endureth all things,

describe more perfectly than he? Could we but
make the motto of his life our own, we should receive from this hour a blessing which would bear
immediate and practical fruit.

   d. Self-will. The best that we can give to God is
our own will. "I have given God my best strength,
but it is still difficult for me to give Him my own will,"
a worker in God's Kingdom said to me recently.
"Then you have not given God your best strength, if
you still have your own will," I replied. The greatest

sacrifice a person can bring to God is his will. God has no pleasure in any other sacrifice as long as we hold fast to our will. "In whole burnt offering—and sacrifices for sin thou hadst no pleasure: Then said I, Lo, I am come . . . to do thy will, O God!" (Heb. 10:6-7). Not offerings does God desire of us, but our will. The question Paul first addressed to Jesus was: "Lord, what wilt thou?" True conversion certainly does not consist in anything else but the resolution to give up one's own will once for all and in all things to do what God wills. And our whole life-task consists, not in doing this or that for God, nor in giving Him this or that, but in *doing God's will.*

There is so much of self-will in our work for the Lord, and, even in our prayers! We make plans, lay them before God and say: "See, dear Lord, I would be glad to do this for Thee. Subscribe to it!" Nay, rather let God make the plans, and let yourself be led by God's Spirit in God's ways. The Sermon on the Mount deals with the "deeper cleansing," and it also speaks of cleansing from false prayers. There we are given a prayer-pattern which reads, "Thy will be done on earth as it is in heaven." James does not say "if the Lord permits," but "if the Lord will" (James 4:15). There is a vast difference.

There are also differences between *subjecting* myself to God's will, and *giving* myself up to it, and *doing it with joy.* The Lamb teaches us to do God's will with joy. He shows us that it is only for the purpose of doing God's will that we have received a will. Gethsemane is both the deepest and the highest point in the Savior's life, and there He said, "Father, not my will." "For the joy that was set before him he endured the cross" (Heb. 12:2). It was because His Father willed it. In all things He said, "Yea, Father, for so it is well-pleasing in thy sight." He willed what God willed. He never had a thought or a wish which was not in perfect accord with the Father's will. This was His "yoke" (Matt. 11:29); therefore He could rejoice in a complete, undisturbed rest. And He invites us also to take His yoke upon us in order that we may find rest for our souls. "I rest on a threefold pillow," says Pearson, "namely, God's boundless love, His wisdom, and His power." For him God's will was synonymous with these three, and in them he found rest.

The people of Israel took their self-will along from Egypt; therefore they could not enter into God's rest (Heb. 3:11). To will something which God does not will, causes inner disturbance, restlessness, pain, and separation from God. From self-will comes self-centeredness, and from this, frequently, a distracted mind. Self-centeredness has brought many more than we think into the insane asylums. Self-will is a disturber of the peace not only in home and society, but also in the heart. How God regards self-will we read in I Samuel 15:23, where Samuel says to Saul, "Stubbornness is as idolatry." Saul confused his own will with God's will and said, "I have obeyed the voice of the Lord." Therefore he was rejected. Self-will cost him his kingdom.

e. Self-satisfaction. Yet another form of our own ego is self-satisfaction. In Romans 15:1-3 it says, "Now we that are strong ought to bear the infirmities of the weak, and *not to please ourselves*. . . . For Christ also pleased not himself." According to these words, self-satisfaction has its roots in our imagining that we are able to do all things. Peter had given up his fishing and could say, "We have forsaken all!" But himself and his own power he had not forsaken. He learned this only after his fall. Someone has said, "Even as our self-righteousness is put to shame by our conversion, and we receive the *righteousness of Christ*, so also, sooner or later, must our own strength be put to shame in order that the *power of Christ may remain in us.*" Would God's children but understand that their own strength is one of their worst enemies! Could the workers in God's kingdom but see that their own power is the greatest hindrance to their bearing fruit for God! God's power can never be made perfect except through our weakness (II Cor. 12:9).

God's power can, to a certain degree, work alongside and together with our power, but it is not perfected in us until we are made weak in God (I Cor. 1:25). Therefore David says, "My strength is dried up like a potsherd," but "Thou hast girded me with strength." God always leads into His weakness those whom He desires to use. His most perfect Servant He led into the greatest weakness. Deeper than the cross can no one descend, and thither God led His Son.

That Christ was free from all self-pleasing we can best see by comparing Hebrews 1:3 and Isaiah 53:3: "The effulgence of his glory," and "He was despised." The power God gave His Son consisted in His becoming most despised, and the commandment God gave Him was that He should lay down His life (John 10:17-18). Here we have a practical explanation of the well-known words in John 1:12: "As many as received him to them gave he power." The power to lay down life is the "power" of the Lamb. He alone is victorious. Therefore, to be "led further" means nothing else than to be "led deeper down," and when we pray, "Lord, strengthen me," the Holy Spirit intercedes for us and says, "Lord, bow me down!"

Self-satisfaction comes always from the feeling of self-sufficiency and superiority. Where there is impotence there is no self-satisfaction. Why do you judge your brother? Why do you give him up? Why do you complain about him? Why do you seek recognition? Why do you make demands? Why are you ashamed of lowly work? *Because you are pleased with yourself.* Why do you like to talk about yourself? You think highly of yourself. Every word has to be forced out of a criminal when he is to speak about himself. Are we other than pardoned criminals? One can talk about anything else with less danger than about himself. Jesus says concerning Satan, "When he speaketh a lie he speaketh of his own." There is great danger for us in that we lie easily when we speak about our own. Joseph found conceit in his home and among his brethren; therefore he spoke about his own advantages, in which he was not entirely unjustified. But he had to be liberated from this self-satisfaction before God could give him the place which He wanted him to have. He was put in prison, and there God purged and cleansed him from all conceit.

f. Self-exaltation. Self-exaltation is the sixth form of the self-life. "I seek not my own glory," said the Lord. Samson used his God-given strength for himself, instead of using it for God. He pulled out the gate-posts of Gaza and carried them up onto the mountain. With his strength he should have saved Israel, but instead he used it to show his own prowess. Similarly, how often we decorate ourselves and dress ourselves up, by means of that which belongs to God and which should be laid down in His sanctuary! Achan should have consecrated the Babylonian cloak and the wedge of gold to the Lord, but he kept them for his own purposes. We too have often used our clear thinking and our eloquent tongue to demonstrate our own cleverness. Why? Because we do not yet know what glory is. God's glory is always veiled and is visible only to him whose eye God has opened. He allowed His Son to take the form of a servant. The manna was covered with hoar-frost, and over the ark of the covenant was drawn an unsightly badger skin. "The king's daughter within the palace is all glorious" (Ps. 45:13). The glory of man is always something external. God's glory is within, in the secret place. "We saw his glory," says John. This glory he saw in the lowliness of the Son of God. John saw the glory in His humiliation; therefore he could follow Him all the way to the cross, even when all the others fled. When once this glory shines into our hearts, we understand Paul's words in Galatians 6:14: "Far be it from me to glory, save in the cross of our Lord Jesus Christ." Then we seek no other glory than that of the Lamb.

Peter liked to compare himself with others. He says, "We have forsaken all," and "How often shall I forgive my brother?" Everywhere, his self-exaltation shines through. Therefore Jesus also made use of comparisons in that strange meeting by the lakeside, when He asked him, "Lovest thou me more than these?—*more?*" But Peter did not consent to this. He had learned not to compare himself with others. He is glad to be able to say to his Master. *"Thou knowest!"* All that is his own has withered away, for the Spirit of the Lord has blown upon him (Isa. 40:7). When the heart is opened to the blessing of God's Spirit, as that blessing is described in Ezekiel 36, the Spirit lets us first see our uncleanness and then cleanses us from it. What God says in the conclusion of that chapter then becomes true: "Ye shall loathe yourselves." This is the opposite of self-exaltation.

6. The Lamb teaches you to be quiet.

"When he was afflicted he opened not his mouth" (Isa. 53:7). The first thing that one learns in the school of the Lamb is to take up His yoke and be quiet (Matt. 11:29). The Scriptures speak of being *quiet before God, quiet in expectation from God,* and *quiet in God.* Before we speak with God we must have become quiet before Him. When Abraham fell upon his face and was silent, God spoke with him (Gen. 17). In chapters 15 and 16 we see how Abraham spoke and acted, while God was silent—for thirteen whole years. We read in chapter 16, "And Abram was fourscore and six years old, when Hagar bare Ishmael." And in chapter 17:1: "And when Abram was ninety years old and nine, Jehovah appeared to Abram." It was a long time, undoubtedly the most difficult in his life; for there is nothing more difficult for a child of God than the Lord's silence. Then Abraham became silent and permitted God to speak.

By being quiet before God a man becomes quiet in expectation from God. "My soul waiteth in silence for God only," says David in Psalm 62. This is already one step higher. It is to entrust all to Him, to expect all things from Him, to receive all things at His hand; and, back of all, to see the Father. Jesus says, in John 6:37, "All that which the Father giveth me shall come unto me." That is to say, I receive all that He has intended for me. When He wants the sun to shine for me, no one can stand in my way.

Such a soul was Mary, who had learned to be quiet in expectation from God. Not in vain did she sit at Jesus' feet. She had learned one of the most difficult of lessons, namely, *to be silent.* When Martha complained about her, she was quiet until her Master came to her defense. If He had no excuse for her, then neither had she. That she understood the Master better than did any of His disciples, she showed by anointing Him for His burial (John 12). She knew that her Lord must die; He must be offered for the salvation of the world—for hers also. Her Lord, like the grain of wheat, must be placed in the ground and die—otherwise there will be but the single grain. By anointing Him she strengthened Him in this conviction, and said, as it were: "Lord, I understand Thy way. Just as the whole house is now filled with the odor of the ointment, so shall Thy death be a 'savour of life' for the world; even as I have given Thee the best that I had, so also, in a far higher degree, wilt Thou give me the best Thou hast. Even as I now pour out the fragrant nard, so will countless others come and do the same, when Thou, by Thy death, hast prepared the way for them." Thus to be understood and encouraged on the way to His death was very refreshing for our Lord.

But what does Judas do? He demands, "To what purpose is this waste?" Waste? Was this a waste? In response, Mary remains silent and awaits the Master's reply. And He defends her, saying,

"She hath wrought a good work upon me. Verily I say unto you, Wheresoever this gospel shall be preached in the whole world, that also which this woman hath done shall be spoken of for a memorial of her." And she is worthy of being remembered, and of having us learn from her today what it is to be "quiet in expectation from God."

Yet no one has been as perfectly quiet as the Lamb. He was quiet when He had no place to lay His head, quiet when there was a Judas among His disciples, quiet in the garden of Gethsemane, quiet upon the cross, *quiet in God!* The highest development is reached when our will, our wishes, and our desires are wholly at one with God's, when He even creates our expectations within us, as we read in Psalm 62:5: "My expectation is from him." Here the soul has entered into the Sabbath rest, the rest in God. Here it feeds on a quietness which, like the depths of the sea, cannot be reached or troubled by any storm. "We drink water from Lake Constance," said a friend to me recently. "Even when it becomes muddy?" I asked him. "At the depth of fifty meters it never becomes muddy, and we have our mains so deep," he answered. Oh, let us strive to enter deeply into fellowship with Jesus, and we shall enjoy "quietness and confidence forever" (Isa. 32:17).

7. The Lamb teaches you to suffer.

"He was made perfect through suffering," says

the Epistle of the Hebrews. That is, through suffering He becomes a perfect Savior. He would not have been this through His words, deeds, and miracles, but became such through suffering. Peter says, "We also are called to suffer." There are wounds that can be healed only by wounds. I read recently about a young man in Baden who allowed a large piece of skin to be taken from his body in order that his sister's burns might be healed. "If thine enemy hunger, feed him; if he thirst, give him to drink; for in so doing thou shalt heap coals of fire upon his head." Permit yourself to be wounded by your enemy, and your wounds will heal his wounds. Concerning Jesus we read, "In that he himself suffered, he is able to succor." He who has suffered can help other sufferers (Ps. 105:17-22).

The men of the Bible had their school of suffering—one in silent waiting, another in prison, one in exile among mountains and caves, another in the desert. Someone has said, "We are wounded in order that we may learn from the great Physician how to bind up wounds and give aid. God visits us with trials in order to teach us to carry the burdens of others. We ourselves must first go to school before we can be teachers of others." We, too, must bear the yoke of suffering and taste the bitter waters in order to be made perfect through suffering. To the equipment of a disciple belongs not only an open ear and the "tongue of the learned," but also a back which permits itself to be smitten and a face which does not hide itself from shame and spitting (Isa. 50). The devil hates most those who are willing to suffer. He knows much better than we what blessings suffering can bring to us and to others. Jesus had His fiercest battle with him in Gethsemane, where He made His decision to go to His death. When we examine our life with this thought in mind, we discover that Satan's attacks were fiercest when we decided to be silent and to suffer. In John 15:2 Jesus says, "Every branch that beareth fruit, he cleanseth it, that it may bring forth more fruit." And the Father, the Gardener, cleanses most often through suffering. Very frequently His pruning-knife is pain.

The Bible speaks of four kinds of suffering: *the suffering of punishment, the suffering of trial, the suffering of cleansing, and suffering for Christ's sake.* Miriam's leprosy was a punishment, the purpose of which was to free her from a spirit of judgment. Israel's wandering in the wilderness was a trial; it was to reveal what was in their hearts. Trials should lead to the endurance of trial, in order that it may be seen whether the heart is honest, whether the soul clings to the Lord—whether we really *are* or only *seem* to be. Joseph's suffering in prison and Daniel's stay in the lions' den were not temptations for them. Their suffering was a cleansing fire. Into this God leads His dearest children. Only he who

has endured testing can be cleansed. Because both
Joseph and Daniel were faithful, this suffering came
upon them. It was faithfulness that brought Joseph
into prison and Daniel into the lions' den. If one
form of suffering after another comes upon your
brother, do not say too quickly: "He must have committed some great wrong." *You* perhaps cannot yet
bear sufferings; therefore God must shield you from
them. Concerning the best and most perfect of the
sons of men, it is said: *"It pleased the Lord to bruise
him"* (Isa. 53:10). The chief thing about the answer-
ing of prayer is not that we can say that we have
prayed for this or for that. It is rather that God has
answered our questions, including also this one,
"Why do I suffer? What is the meaning of my present suffering for me?"

Suffering enlarges the heart in that it creates
sympathy. No one has so much sympathy for the
poor as he who has himself been poor. No one has
such profound sympathy for the sick as he who has
long since had to give up the precious boon of good
health. It is said that of all evils, an unfeeling heart is
the worst. By sympathy is not meant merely feeling
or expressing some sympathetic emotion or other; it
is rather that deep and heartfelt participation which
feels another's burden and need as much as he
himself does. Moses, Ezra, and Nehemiah had this
kind of sympathy. They did not hold themselves
above the need of their people, but placed themselves under their burden. They made the guilt of

the people their own and brought it before God. Such souls often support a whole congregation, which otherwise really could not survive. They are pillars in the house of God. They are always in their place; they do not speak loudly in the meetinghall, but they pray. They pray for each individual who comes in through the door, and gladness fills their hearts when those enter who faithfully follow the Lord. Profound sympathy grips them when someone comes who perhaps has recently fallen or gone away from God.

8. The Lamb teaches you to be obedient.

"He was obedient" (Phil. 2:8). In these three words the Holy Spirit summarizes the whole life of the Savior. They mark the highest point in His whole life-story. His miracles were great, His word shall never pass away; but greater even than these was His obedience. It was His meat to do the Father's will. What Jesus revealed to the world was His obedience to the Father. A better gift or a more effective sermon we do not possess. If we can show our neighbor our obedience to God, we have given him the best. "What is the result of sanctification?" a brother asked recently. What was the result in the life of the Lamb? We find it in these words: "Becoming obedient even unto death, yea, the death of the cross" (Phil. 2:8). God could require of Him what was most difficult, and He did it with joy. *False* sanc-

tification leads one to think highly of himself; he speaks of the experience he has had, of the development to which he has attained, and so on. Biblical sanctification brings a person down into the dust, annihilates every "grace of the soul," and leaves only one desire: to be pleasing to God. Sanctification is nothing but obedience (Gen. 22, Phil. 2). When Jesus had reached the deepest depths, in the presence of the cross, He spoke of sanctification. "For their sakes I sanctify myself, that they themselves also may be sanctified in truth." When we sanctify ourselves thus even to the cross, to sacrifice, and when with our Savior we descend to the lowest place, then will also others around us "be sanctified in truth." Even if we cannot be anything else but examples of obedience for our fellowmen, this in itself is exceedingly great. Nothing attracts men and leads them so much to reflection as a person who walks in obedience.

Obedience gives power. The source of Christ's victory, the secret of His power, and of ours, lies in obedience. Therein we find our greatest liberty. Only he who is free can be the servant of all. He can also help others to find liberty. In an obedient heart there is a way prepared for God. There are many Christians who always seek pleasure and satisfaction for themselves. These have not yet learned that only obedient children are happy children. That which in truth brings abiding happiness is nothing else than obedience toward God. For a healthy soul there is only one thing that counts—to be obedient. To "do God's will" strengthens us and becomes our "meat"—much more than does puzzling over God's Word and trying to understand it.

Why have so many of God's lambs so little assurance of salvation? Why are their souls not satisfied with the peace of God? God gives us the answer in Isaiah 48:18: "Oh, that thou hadst hearkened to my commandments! Then had thy peace been as a river, and thy righteousness as the waves of the sea." People say, "I lack faith. I have too little faith; therefore I have no assurance of salvation, no peace." But in most instances it is not faith which is lacking, for even with a trembling hand one can receive costly gifts. It is rather obedience which is lacking. There is something in their lives which they will not let go, and which hinders the Holy Spirit from giving them the assurance that they are God's children. I knew a man who for nine whole months could not believe in Christ's atonement, for the simple reason that he himself was not willing to be forgiving. He might have prayed and struggled for nine years or ninety more, if he had not taken care of that matter. There is a difference between putting forth an effort to believe that I am saved and having the witness of the Holy Spirit that I am saved. *No one who is disobedient to God can have confidence in Him. Confidence is a result of obedience.* For Jesus it was entirely natural to have confidence in

God since obedience was a matter of course for Him.

It is not enough to believe that I am saved. I must also walk in such a way that the salvation which I have appropriated in faith can be realized. This is the way of obedience. Recently a friend wrote to me somewhat as follows: "It seems to me that one of the greatest hindrances to the consistent following of Jesus lies in this, that we constantly speak about *acts of faith* and therefore little about the *continued growing Christian life.* We speak of the fulness of the Spirit as an act, of baptism as an act of obedience, of being kept in fellowship with God, after having surrendered wholly unto Him, as an act, and so on. This is a great mistake. Just as little as a straw consists of individual joints, can our life with the Lord consist of individual acts. The joints in the straw are not the chief thing; they merely serve to fasten the new parts. We fear the continuous experience of the way, and therefore we speak about the individual acts. Then we do not need to enter into self-denial, into death, into the struggle, and we remain in the flesh." In the twenty-fifth Psalm David prays for three things:

1. Show me thy way, O Lord.
2. Guide me in thy way.
3. Lord, teach me thy way.

It is not enough that we *know* the way; we must also walk in it step by step, and from time to time we must be instructed by the Lord in order to be able to walk in the right way.

9. The Lamb teaches you to have faith.

"He trusted in God," cried His enemies. Jesus kept His faith in God all the way to His death on the cross. In the deepest darkness He relied upon His Father. When He stepped down into the Jordan and presented Himself as a participant in the guilt of man's sins, and when on Mount Tabor He decided to drink the cup of suffering to its last drop, heaven opened each time, and the good pleasure of God shone visibly over Him. But when He came to the end of the Way of Love and carried God's will to completion upon the cross, heaven was dark and impenetrable. In Gethsemane there was only an angel, and by the cross just a disciple and some women, so that the enemies with apparent truth could say, "See how much confidence in God has helped Him!" Thus it can come to pass that just where we seek most of all to do God's will, we least of all experience His good pleasure. Think of Daniel and his friends! In this way it is soon seen whether we seek *Him* or His *gifts*.

To put one's trust in God in difficult and dark days is quite different from following Him in days of sunshine. We read in Genesis 15, "Abraham believed in Jehovah and he reckoned it to him for righteousness." But then came a time of testing. Abraham sought light, but darkness covered him; he sought the face of God, and terror fell upon him. He brought to God the offering He had commanded him to bring, and waited for God to come and receive it; but instead, the birds of prey came down upon it. Only when it became *dark* did God come. And then came the solution: "Thy seed shall sojourn in a land that is not theirs—but thou shalt go to thy fathers in peace." It was a difficult trial, but Abraham was not shaken in his confidence in God. He rested in the assurance that God was faithful.

We have had similar experiences, have we not? When we believed ourselves to be near the goal we had set for ourselves, God suddenly snatched it forward a long distance. When we hoped that we had overcome the hardest trial, a still more difficult one came. Perhaps you have surrendered your sick body to God for healing. You wanted to put your confidence in Him and let Him alone have the glory. You have brought your offering today, expecting improvement tomorrow, but matters only become worse. Instead of the Lord's receiving your offering and establishing the covenant with you, doubts come which lead you to take your offering back again. It is clear, of course, that God does not care whether one depends upon Him or not. But only wait! If you hold out in patience, you will win a great victory, both for yourself and for others. Do you know why the penitent thief has become such an attractive figure and has become a guide to light and peace for so many thousands? Because he *be-*

lieved just in the hour when all round about his God was dark. It is difficult for us to believe when all is dark around us; but the robber believed in spite of the darkness. It was certainly not easy for him to see the Son of God in this dying Jesus, and to call this despised man his Lord. Only the Lamb there beside him gave him such confidence. He does not *teach* people confidence, but *gives* it, just as one does not teach comfort, but gives it. The thief has given his confidence to hundreds and thousands of hearts. Go to a deathbed where a human being struggles in the agonies of sin and death. Set forth the plan of salvation to him in the most striking words. It will not reach his heart. But say, "Remember the dying thief," and behold, light shines into his soul and confidence and comfort begin to dwell there. Despair not, therefore, if there is darkness about you, for the Lord dwelleth also "in the thick darkness" (I Kings 8:12). Honor God with your confidence. "He trusted in God" means also that *He had His sufficiency in God.* Had we but learned this, we should be free from hundreds of sorrows, from cares and much fear. God all; I naught! What need I more? What then can harm or disturb me?

10. The Lamb teaches you to work.

"He shall see of the travail of his soul and shall be satisfied," we read of Him in Isaiah 53. There is such a thing as soul-work, and this the Lamb practised more than anyone else. God can permit us to see things which call forth bitter tears; for when we take upon us the yoke of Christ, we find that every single soul has eternal worth. Oh, how hard and unsympathetic we are! How often we forget that our work concerns immortal souls, that it is a work of eternal value! While thousands of souls rush onward toward eternal death with its closed portal, its eternal chains and endless woe, we stand indifferent, powerless, and heartless, because we seek only our own. There are few who can say as did Jeremiah when his people discarded the law of the Lord: "Mine eye poureth down, and ceaseth not, without any intermission" (Lam. 3:49). Jesus wept over Jerusalem, and sorrowed over the people. Therefore people also streamed toward Him. Only a compassionate heart wins hearts. There is a compassion to which no sinner, in the end, can close his eyes, a compassion which is stronger than words. Let us learn it of Him.

The sixth chapter of II Corinthians, where Paul speaks of his work, opens with the words, "Working together." With whom? With God! And how does God work? Paul gives the answer in chapter 5:21: "Him who knew no sin he made to be sin on our behalf." We can never understand what this involves, but can you feel it? God has *made His Son to be sin!* Can you feel what it was for the Son to be made sin for others—for one's enemies! Thus God works! Paul says, "I work as does God, I give the dearest I have; even as He did, I too am not afraid to give my life." Read through II Corinthians 6 and see how far

Paul condescended, how completely he offered himself, what a life of self-denial he lived. Do not say too readily that you are a worker in God's Kingdom. Can you say: I am a worker together with God? Is it duty or love which constrains you? Do you work in order to lose your life or to find it?

The Bible usually shows us our Master in two aspects: as a *Servant* and as a *Lamb*. He came to serve, but His service became more and more that of *bearing*. From the form of a servant was born the form of a Lamb. We observe the mileposts on His way of service, and after each of them the way becomes more steep and narrow. The circle of disciples becomes smaller, because the goal becomes more definite. And when He turned His face toward the cross, He was followed by only one. The others forsook Him. They could probably understand that He was to be a Servant, but not that He must be a Lamb. The Holy Spirit led Him onward, step by step, and with every step He descended lower—all the way to the death on the cross. The nearer He came to the cross, the clearer the cross shone before Him, and the more clearly could the form of the Lamb be seen in the form of the Servant. In a like manner does the Lord lead His followers. Their service becomes more and more one of bearing. He leads them from the outer court into the sanctuary where God alone is.

The Goal of the Way . . .

And I heard as it were the voice of a great multitude, and as the voice of many waters, and as the voice of mighty thunders, saying, Hallelujah: for the Lord our God, the Almighty, reigneth. Let us rejoice and be exceeding glad, and let us give the glory unto him: for the marriage of the Lamb is come, and his wife hath made herself ready. And it was given unto her that she should array herself in fine linen, bright and pure: for the fine linen is the righteous acts of the saints.—Rev. 19:6-8.

We have spoken about "The Way in the Footprints of the *Lamb*." Now let us look into the *goal* of that way. Only he who has a goal before him will hasten onward and with joy overcome the difficulties of the way.

The destiny of the Christian is the *visible union with the Lamb.* In Ephesians 5:31-32, we read: " . . . and the two shall become one flesh. This mystery is great: but I speak in regard of Christ and of the church." Consequently, to be "one flesh" with Him is more than to be one spirit with Him. Two

73

young people become engaged, because they are of one spirit; but both look forward to the day when they shall stand by each other's side as man and wife. So is it with Christ and the Church. The Church longs for the moment when as the Bride, she shall stand with a glorified body at His side.

When the Scriptures speak about the eternal destiny of the believers, it gives them two names: "a kingdom of priests" (Rev. 1:6) and "the wife of the Lamb" (Rev. 19:7). This has not yet been fulfilled in us. At the most we are this in a spiritual sense; but this is not the perfected state. A merely spiritual interpretation, especially of these two names, is a great hindrance to the coming of the Kingdom of God. We must learn to understand that we have to do with more than personal development, that we must not stop with our experiences, that spiritual *enjoyment* is not sufficient: we must press on to something much higher. Not long ago someone said to me: "Only recently has it become clear to me that we are not concerned only with personal salvation. Conversion is an experience; the forgiveness of sins is an actuality; peace with God brings deep joy. But all these things, which we must have experienced and must possess, are not themselves the goal, but only the means of attaining to it. Our destiny is a visible union with the Son of God. We must therefore not stop here, lest we be numbered among the foolish virgins. For through all this the Kingdom of God is not furthered to any great extent—and this, of course, is of first significance."

We ourselves are saved in order to help in the salvation of others, and this salvation includes not only the lost world but the whole creation which groans in pain. When Paul speaks of the *proclamation of the Gospel*, he enlarges the circle to include all men; but when he speaks about *salvation*, he makes the circle yet larger and includes within it the whole groaning creation (Rom. 8:19-23). The travail of creation does not concern God's ear, but ours. The earnest expectation of creation is not for the revealing of the Son of God but for the revealing of the *sons* of God. Thereby is the redemption of creation laid upon our shoulders and written as a debt on our account. This gives us a larger vision of our task and tells us that our ultimate goal cannot be "to come to heaven" in order to rest forever there.

He who stops here does not understand his calling as a Christian and does not know what the real issues are in our time and for the future. We are all members of Christ's body; He Himself is the Head and from Him "every creature in heaven and on earth and under the earth" awaits a complete salvation (Rev. 5). We may stop only where Christ, our Head, stops, and He is finished only when He has laid all things under the Father's feet, in order that God may be all in all (I Cor. 15:20-28). Until that time our blessedness consists in serving (Rev. 22:3), that together with the Son we may bring a lost world into subjection to the Father. Thus will the Kingdom of God come, as Jesus has taught us to pray in the Lord's Prayer. The final and perfect state is, therefore, not the "Kingdom of the Son" but the "Kingdom of the Father," for this is the Father's house. The Kingdom of God has two aspects: an earthly and a heavenly. The earthly one is the "Kingdom of the Spirit" in which we now live, and the "Kingdom of the Son" which is fast approaching; the heavenly one is the "Kingdom of the Father," where *He* is Father and all are His children.

God never gives up, but always begins anew. Every time things seem to go backward, the Lord nevertheless wins a step forward, as we see in the history of the Kingdom of God. Jesus began with twelve men. To them He gave His Holy Spirit. According to Acts 15:14, they were given the task of "gathering a people for his name" among the Gentiles. When this is completed, the Lord will come again in order to begin anew with this saved people and by them "proclaim light" (Acts 26:23) to those who yet sit in darkness and the shadow of death. It is a question of "Firstfruits" (James 1:18), a group who can assist in the work of salvation.

According to the Scriptures, it is not *now* the work of the Holy Spirit to convert the world, but to *choose out a people from the world.* In Acts 15 we read about the first general meeting of the servants of Christ. There they agreed as to the lines along which they should work, and as to the goal they should seek to attain. The goal was clearly and definitely marked out. This concerns also us. Every work that is not done according to these directions cannot be confirmed by the Holy Spirit. It is not enough that we give people guidance as to conversion to Christ; we ourselves must *lead* them to Christ. Then we are doing a work according to the instructions given by the Holy Spirit, a work which has significance for the Kingdom of God. The conversion and life of many believers have value only for their own personal salvation, but not for the Kingdom of God. There is a difference between "dying saved"—as we sometimes say—and serving God as a king and priest in the coming Kingdom! Paul says to the Corinthians that he is "jealous over them with a godly jealousy" in order that he may "present them as a pure virgin to Christ" (II Cor. 11:2). To the Philippians he says that if he does not attain to this goal, he has *run and labored in vain* (Phil. 2:15, 16). Oh, how many of our laborers, seen from this viewpoint, will on that day receive the mark: *In vain!* Yes, many a work will be seen to have been a great mistake!

Thus we can understand why, in spite of all the work done, so little is accomplished. The seal of the Spirit is lacking! And more than that, because one does not work according to the plan of the Holy Spirit, one grieves the Holy Spirit by the very work one desires to carry out for God. For in the light of their context, the words, "Grieve not the Spirit," point forward to the day of salvation—that is, to the coming of the Lord. Every member of the body of Christ who halts, and does not allow himself to be led on to perfection, grieves the Holy Spirit, the Masterbuilder of the body of Christ. This hinders the development of the whole body. When I sin today, I sin not only against God and against myself, but I sin against the whole body of Christ, of which I am a member. Thus, too, we are to understand the deeper meaning of that word: "Whether one member suffereth, all the members suffer with it" (I Cor. 12:26).

We must not stop with "assurance of salvation"; for this, according to Hebrews 6, belongs to the beginnings of the Christian life, but not to the full growth. There is something much deeper than assurance of salvation, and that is *the consciousness that we belong together with Christ.* We are called and chosen, predestined from eternity for the Son. There is a great difference between these two things: whether I consider myself as one who is "found" or as one who is "chosen." There is something accidental about being found, but when I am chosen, I acknowledge the eternal grace of God over me. Scripture designates us *called* and *elected,* and we must always stand on Scriptural ground. When a person is converted, he begins the life of fellowship with God; but God's beginning with that person reaches back much farther, all the way into eternity. In Ephesians 1:4 we read that we are "chosen in him before the foundation of the world." And in John 6:37 Jesus says: "All that which the Father giveth me shall come unto me." If I have come to Jesus, it proves to me that I am among those blessed souls whom the Father has given to the Son. If we have understood this truth of our belonging together with the Son of God, we shall do three things:

A. *For the first time we shall thank God from the depths of our heart that we have been born as human beings*—a thing which perhaps many of us until this hour have never done. Then the moment has come when the love of God is richly shed abroad in our hearts. We are touched with that spiritual nobility which lifts us above the joys and sorrows of our earthly life.

B. *We no longer draw the Word of God down to the level of our experience,* as we so long have been doing. We permit the ideals and goals of Scripture to stand, and strive toward them, as Paul says, "that I may lay hold on that for which also I was laid hold on by Christ Jesus." For we do not receive the Word of God merely with reference to *our* feelings, but with reference to what *God* feels and has need of.

C. *We live as strangers in this world.* Its pleasures no longer attract us, and its sufferings no longer make us afraid. When Rebekah had seen her bridegroom, Isaac, she dismounted hurriedly from her beast and veiled her face. From that moment she did not want to please any other, did not want to be attractive to any other than to him. Such will also be our attitude when it has become clear to us that we belong to *Him.*

He That Cometh . . .

Cast not away therefore your boldness, which hath great recompense of reward. For ye have need of patience, that, having done the will of God, ye may receive the promise. For yet a very little while, he that cometh shall come, and shall not tarry.—Heb. 10:35-37.

"Der Herr bricht ein um Mitternacht, jetzt ist noch alles still"* we read in an old song. When Zinzendorf wrote this song, more than a hundred years ago, those words were true. But praise be to God, now all things are no longer quiet. Even if God's people on the whole have little expectation of the Lord's return, or interest in it, there is, nevertheless, a group who have awakened and who "wait for his Son from heaven" (I Thess. 1:10).

The great event to which God's children look forward is the coming of the Son of God, not the outpouring of the Holy Spirit. In the New Testament, among the apostolic writers, we find no ex-

---

*The Lord will come at midnight,
As yet all earth is still.

hortation to wait for an outpouring of the Spirit. The apostles did not prepare their congregations for the coming of the Holy Spirit but for the coming of the Lord Jesus. That which has led many sincere children of God to wait for an outpouring of the Spirit is the spiritual poverty among God's people in general, and the conviction that as God's people are today, we shall never be able to get through the difficult times which are just before us; we must receive a special revelation of God from heaven. This is certainly true, but that revelation will be not an outpouring of the Holy Spirit but a *taking away* of those who have permitted themselves to be molded and liberated by the Spirit that they might be ready to be caught up to meet the Lord. This terrifies those who remain behind, but will at the same time give them strength. From that moment the Revelation will become an open book for those who are left behind, and each one will be determined to be faithful even unto death during the short time that remains.

The apostles do not speak of the Holy Spirit's "coming" but of "receiving" the Holy Spirit. Jesus received the Holy Spirit when He stepped down into the Jordan, thus presenting Himself as a participant in humanity's guilt. He received the Holy Spirit in the form of a *dove*. If we go down this way to the Jordan and meet the Holy Spirit with a trusting heart, then nothing will any longer hinder us from receiving a deeper blessing of the Spirit. In our time the question is not of an *outpouring of the Spirit* but of *spiritual ripening.* The closer we come to the harvest time, the greater is the heat and the less is the rain. Do not wait for special blessing; for Peter says: "His divine power hath granted unto us all things that pertain unto life and godliness" (II Pet. 1:3).

The coming of God's Son is the real hope of the believers, as we read in Acts 1:11, Titus 2:13, I Cor. 1:7, Phil. 3:20, and many other places. The early Christians constantly looked forward to it. The Church in its first love waited for its Lord. How often too Jesus Himself and His apostles admonished us to wait for His coming and to hasten to meet Him! The return of the Lord is not a theme with which certain specialists occupy themselves, but it is the great theme of Scripture and it must also become ours. We are all deeply aware of the fact that our congregations need a spiritual renewal. "How can this take place?" I asked a missionary. "When the hope of the Lord's return becomes living in our congregations," he answered. Seen in the light of Scripture, this is the best answer. Paul says to the Thessalonians, "Put on for a helmet the hope of salvation." The helmet of hope is surely nothing else but the Living Hope of the Lord's return. As long as this does not live in our hearts, we are lacking an essential piece of the Spirit's armor. Why do so many remain just where they are? Why are so many sensitive, so easily offended, and always feeling themselves forsaken and set aside? They lack the helmet of hope.

Think of a congregation of three hundred in which there were thirty who really were waiting for the Lord. What holiness and what light these could give to a congregation! John says, "Everyone that hath this hope set on him purifieth himself even as he is pure." He that does not have this hope, does not cleanse himself. Those who are really waiting need not be exhorted to cleanse themselves; they do it without outward prompting. They do not need to be urged to press forward, to deny themselves, to humble themselves; they just naturally strive to be like the Lamb. They do not cleanse themselves only from *sins but also from themselves*, that is, from their own mind, their own nature, from all that is not of Him, and is not directed toward Him. As long as we do not have *this* Hope, we are really without hope; and the state of such persons is known to us all.

For several years I could not answer this question: *"What is the first love?"* The "first love" could not be what I and others understood by it, for these things the congregation in Ephesus had. It received a tenfold praise, but after this a: "But." "But I have this against thee, that thou didst leave thy first love." The Ephesians had not *lost* but had *left* the first love. What is the first love? As far as I can now understand it, it is the *living hope of Jesus' return*. Ephesus represented the Church during the first centuries: it began to give up the hope of the Heavenly Bridegroom's coming; it forsook its first love.

What would one say of a bride who expected to receive everything from her bridegroom, but not himself? One would say, "Child, you no longer have the right attitude toward your bridegroom; you have forsaken your first love." But, if we are to be entirely honest, we must say: "We cannot forsake the first love, for we have not yet had it!" We are like the princess in the forty-fifth Psalm who was called to the king's side but did not understand the significance of this, and therefore clung to the things at home. It was necessary for the king to call anew and say, "Hearken, O daughter, and consider, and incline thine ear; forget also thine own people, and thy father's house: so will the king desire thy beauty. . . . " May the Lord open our ears to His call and open our eyes to the vision of Himself, so that "the first love" may awaken also in *our* hearts, and we may become a serving and expectant people.

Hitherto many of us have been like the brother who once said: "For many years I have known that I was converted, but I did not know for what purpose. I have long known that I was sealed with the Holy Spirit, but not to what end. But I understood it when I Thess. 1:9-10 and Eph. 4:30 became clear to me: we are converted to serve the true and living God, and to *wait* for His Son from Heaven." This is the purpose of our conversion, and the reward is salvation from "the wrath to come," from the great tribulation which shall come upon the whole world (Rev. 3:10). Those will be saved who have these two marks of a true conversion: service and expectation.

Nothing hinders this salvation except the preparation which makes us ready to receive it. The reason that the Lord cannot yet take His people away from "the wrath" is that they are not yet gathered and prepared for His coming. For when the Lord *now* comes, He does not come to the *world* to *judgment*, but as we are told in Hebrews 9:28: *"Unto salvation for those who wait for him."* In the same verse we read, "He shall appear a second time apart from sin." That is, while at His first coming He *bore* sin, at His last coming He shall *judge* sin, He will then have nothing to do with sin. This coming He does not associate with sin, but with the "saints" and the "glorified ones," as we read in Psalm 16. He comes to His own like the radiant star of morning, quietly, without the sleeping world's being aware of it. "So then let us not sleep, as do the rest, but let us watch and be sober . . . putting on the breastplate of faith and love; and for a helmet, the hope of salvation" (I Thess. 5:6-8).